THE GREAT PHILOSOPHERS

Consulting Editors
Ray Monk and Frederic Raphael

Published in 1999 by
Routledge
29 West 35th Street
New York, NY 10001

First published in 1997 by
Phoenix
A Division of the Orion Publishing Group Ltd.
Orion House
5 Upper Saint Martin's Lane
London WC2H 9EA

10 9 8 7 6 5 4 3 2 1

Library of Congress Cataloging-in-Publication Data

Cartledge, Paul.
    Democritus / Paul Cartledge.
     p. cm.—(The great philosophers : 14)
    Includes bibliographical references.
    ISBN 0-415-92389-1 (pbk.)
    1. Democritus. I. Title. II. Series: Great Philosophers
(Routledge (Firm)) : 14.
B298.C37 1999
182'.7—dc21   99-14466
                                      CIP

DEMOCRITUS

Paul Cartledge

ROUTLEDGE
New York

CONTENTS

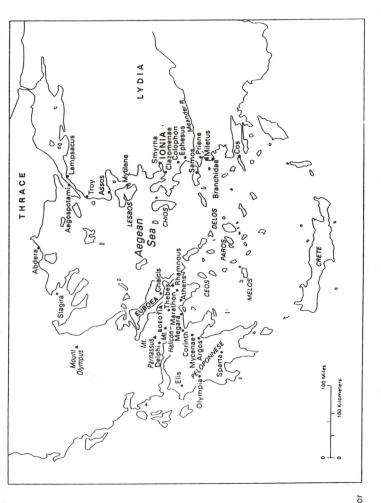

Greece and
Western Asia Minor

In a goal-less caucus race,
Atoms rush through empty space
Or a lunatic dervish dance
From whose whirling, by mere chance
Order somehow comes to birth –
Sky and stars, and this green earth.
Living forms of every kind,
Till at length emergent mind
Gleams for a little while, and then
Things collapse to chaos again.
Old Democritus, how he laughed –
Scheme that's both sublime and daft.

from *Laughing Philosopher/Weeping Philosopher*
by John Heath-Stubbs

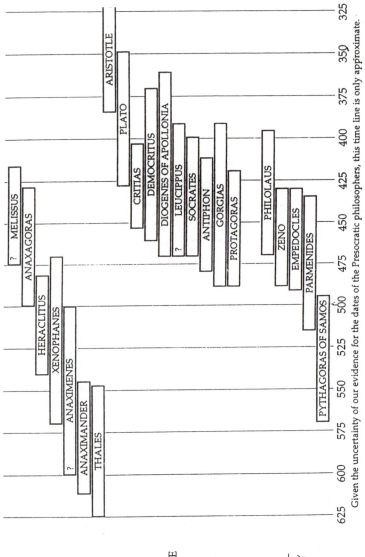

Given the uncertainty of our evidence for the dates of the Presocratic philosophers, this time line is only approximate.

ACKNOWLEDGEMENTS

Frederic Raphael was kind enough to invite this small text. My Cambridge colleague, Professor David Sedley, offered sage advice and bibliographical guidance, especially on the 'void'. My former undergraduate pupil James Warren, another genuine Democritus expert, generously and helpfully commented on earlier drafts. Any remaining infelicities and errors must be attributed to my soul's ill-schooled condition.

To Gabrielle
(*all my own work*)

DEMOCRITUS

Democritus and Atomistic Politics

A BRIEF LIFE AND TIMES

In principle, the matter of which the cosmos is composed is now scientifically established. Yet probably not many people know that, when scientists recently reported the discovery of the 'top quark', they were announcing the completion of a project initiated by the ancient Greeks. One person who would have known that is the late Nobel laureate Erwin Schrödinger:

> Matter is constituted of particles, separated by comparatively large distances; it is embedded in empty space. This notion goes back to Leucippus and Democritus, who lived in Abdera in the fifth century BC. This conception of particles and empty space is retained today ... and not only that, there is complete historical continuity.[1]

Even Schrödinger, though, did not get it all quite right. In Greek *atomon* meant etymologically an entity that could not be cut or divided, *a-tomon*. The indivisibility could notionally have been conceptual rather than physical, but in at least some accounts of Democritus' theory the *atoma* in question are described in physical terms as 'full' (D/K A44, 45, 46).[2] If there is any one thing that marks the crucial *dis*continuity between the ancient Greek enquiry into nature and modern scientific theory and practice, it is the splitting of the atom, by Cockcroft and Walton in Cambridge in 1932, and the discovery through experiment of subatomic particles.

That Democritus lived in the fifth century BC is, however,

as certain as any proposition about the past can be. Yet despite his clearly justified fame in antiquity – Aristotle, his pupil Theophrastus, Epicurus, his companion Metrodorus and the leading Stoics Cleanthes and Sphaerus all devoted treatises to his work – his life is to us practically a closed book. Diogenes Laertius, who compiled a compendious *Lives of the Ancient Philosophers* in the third century of our era, did his best, but the result was inevitably as jejune and unauthoritative as the available materials.[3]

Democritus seems to have lived to a good age by ancient standards, perhaps from about 460 to 385 BC. This was long before Greeks had developed the interest in biography that culminated around AD 100 in Plutarch's *Parallel Lives* of great Greeks and Romans. Democritus lived, moreover, in Abdera, not in Athens, the then centre of the Greeks' and the world's intellectual universe that his younger contemporary Plato (*c.* 427–347 BC) described patriotically as the 'city hall of Wisdom'. Abdera was a settlement on the northern shore of the Aegean, founded by Ionian Greeks from Teos in Asia Minor in about 540 BC. By the time of Demosthenes (384–322 BC) it had acquired an opposite reputation for stupidity and foolishness, unjustly no doubt. At any rate, here Democritus was born and is said to have held public office, a report possibly confirmed by coins bearing the legend 'in the term of Democritus' and dated around 414 BC. Unlike his fellow northerner Aristotle (born 384 BC), Democritus did not choose to emigrate southwards to Athens. He did, however, like his compatriot and older contemporary Protagoras, visit the violet-crowned city. His reception was in his own alleged words jarringly different: 'I came to Athens and no one knew me.' That was presumably after the circulation there of at least some of his writings in the later part of the fifth century, but before the

4

establishment in the early fourth century of Greece's first permanent schools of higher learning, those of Isocrates (436–338 BC) and Plato.

Democritus had a reputation for conducting extensive travel outside as well as inside Greece. One late source drawn upon by Diogenes Laertius has him travelling not only to Egypt to visit the priests and learn geometry – that was more or less *de rigueur* – but also to Persia, to Babylonia (to visit the Chaldaeans) and down as far as the Red Sea. Another source reported his alleged claim that 'he would rather discover a single causal explanation [*aitiologia* – perhaps a word actually coined by Democritus] than become Great King of Persia' (D/K B118). That remark would very likely have been based on first-hand experience of the mighty Persian Empire, which had been founded in *c.* 550 BC and stretched ultimately from the Punjab to the east Mediterranean. On the other hand, the recent historical novel that gave Democritus a Persian connection by marriage was rather stretching the point.[4]

Nevertheless, to give Democritus an oriental connection is not only politically correct in terms of today's academic discourse but also accurate in intellectual–historical terms. Early Greek science did develop and flower in close association with and sometimes strict dependence on ideas that reached Greek thinkers from the Middle East, especially Babylonia, Persia and Egypt. On the other hand, the Greeks non-mythical, non-religious enquiry into nature was their own invention. It was concerned at first to discover what the non-human cosmos was made of, rather than how or why it was the way it was.[5]

The intellectual breakthrough is generally supposed to have been launched in Ionia, part of western Turkey today. The earliest great name on record is that of Thales, a regular member of the Greeks' own list of Seven Sages. He hailed from Miletus, as did Anaximander and Anaximenes; Xenophanes was from Colophon, and Heraclitus from Ephesus. Together, the careers of these men spanned the sixth century BC, by the end of which Greek Ionia was a part of the Persian Empire. Between them, they speculated on the ultimate constituent of matter, predicted eclipses, discovered and correctly interpreted fossils, drew a map of the world, and denied that the cosmos had been created, even by gods.

The suspension of belief in the divine, or at any rate the removal of the divine as conventionally (mythically) conceived from explanatory hypotheses, was a crucial move common to them all – regardless of their own personal religious beliefs and practices. Just how extraordinary that move was requires firm emphasis. The claim attributed to Thales himself that 'everything was full of gods' was a notion on which ordinary, non-intellectual Greeks habitually acted and around which indeed they organized much of their daily life. Yet from Thales onwards for the next couple of hundred years the distinction and separation of what we would call religion and science were vital to the intellectual project of the enquiry into nature. That was perhaps the essential core of what is sometimes referred to as the Greek Enlightenment.

Plato, almost inevitably, begged to disagree. And it is thanks chiefly to Plato that the scientists and philosophers known collectively as the Presocratics, of whom Democritus was the last, have almost without exception not survived to address us in their own right. For it was a major part of Plato's purpose, showing himself in this respect at any rate fully representative of the agonistic or competitive character of all ancient Greek intellection, to put out of

6

court and drive from the market all earlier philosophers apart from Socrates – or at any rate his representation of 'Socrates'. This aim he achieved with near-total success. Of Protagoras, for example, we have just six, mainly very short examples of what may have been his *ipsissima verba*; in fact, he is paradoxically best known through the *Protagoras*, the Socratic dialogue Plato named after him. As for Democritus, Plato notoriously fails altogether to mention either him or his writings, though (especially in the *Timaeus*) he arguably betrays knowledge of them, if only indirectly. And although we have many more than six 'fragments' attributable to Democritus – almost 300 in all, the two main ancient collections together comprising some 200 – they are still few and rather lamentable when set beside the huge list of complete works attributed to him that Diogenes Laertius dutifully lists.

Nor can we ever be sure that these alleged quotations by later doxographers, commentators and anthologists are in fact verbatim; in style at least they vary enormously, from the ornate and even verbose to the sparely gnomic. In the case of those attributed not to Democritus but to 'Democrates' it is of course strictly an article of faith that they are his at all (though the spelling mistake, if that is what it is, would have been an easy one). The same holds, *a fortiori*, for the work that goes under the title 'Anonymus Iamblichi' ('the Anonymous Author of Iamblichus', so called because the text is embedded in a work of the fourth-century AD doxographer Iamblichus). Nevertheless, despite all these provisos, scholars seem to be agreed that enough of the right, authentically Democritean stuff survives to base at least quite firmly tentative conclusions upon it.

Apart from the fragility of the evidential base, the other

main point about Democritus' *oeuvre* that needs emphasizing at the outset is its diversity. Today he is ineluctably identified with Atomism, or even seen as an atomist *pur sang*, and therefore assigned to the domain of Science. But in ancient Greece, as in the Renaissance and indeed up to the nineteenth century, knowledge (the root meaning of Latin *scientia*) was conceived rather as a unified spectrum, not the sum of discrete, compartmentalized 'knowledges'. And Democritus was a leading player in all the then recognized forms of knowledge and intellection, an abstract theorist of the very highest order but also one with an eminently practical bent. He was, therefore, in our terms not only a physicist but also (among other things) a cosmologist, geologist, medical writer and ethical and political philosopher, and, it will be argued here, an original and important one too.

Given the state of the extant evidence, indeed, who are we to say whether he might not himself have seen his 'scientific' work as fundamental but yet subordinated ultimately to an overarching and overriding ethical–political project rather than as an independent end and goal in itself? At any rate, the main point to register is that his thought, or philosophy, was not narrowly confined within the sphere of physical science. If it is with his physics (the original Greek word means 'matters to do with nature') that we shall begin, that is because it is for his physics that Democritus is today most famed.

PHYSICS AND EPISTEMOLOGY

Descartes' *cogito ergo sum* lies at the root of all rational philosophical speculation. It was his (flawed) response to the foundational question 'of what can one be certain?' In Democritus' day, thinkers were no less exercised by such epistemological dilemmas, and the dominant tendency among the Presocratics, especially the Sophists (not a school, but a movement, of quite disparate thinkers), was to err on the side of relativism or even scepticism.[7] At the opposite extreme of antithesis – it was characteristic of Greek mentality and thought to pose issues in polar terms – there stood the absolutist–monist Parmenides of Elea. Plato understandably regarded the latter as a progenitor of his own doctrine that knowledge of the truth was both possible and almost tautologously necessary, since knowledge must be of that which really is, and that which really is is both absolutely true and impervious to flux and change. Between the Sophists and Parmenides, Democritus occupied a characteristically middling – and moderate – position. On the one hand, knowledge of absolute truth was in his view not on offer:

A man must learn on this principle that he is far removed from the truth. (D/K B6; C/M 23)

Yet it will be clear that to know how each thing is in reality is a puzzle. (D/K B8; B p. 253)

We know nothing truly, for the truth lies hidden in the depth. (D/K B117)

On that point Democritus agreed with the Sophists. On the other hand, empirical evidence of the senses, as interpreted within his atomist schema, gave scope for advancing beyond mere relativist conventionalism:

> We know nothing truly about anything, but for each of us opining is a rearrangement [of soul atoms]. (D/K B7)

> In truth we know nothing unerringly, but only as it changes according to the disposition of our body, and of the things that enter into it and impinge on it. (D/K B9)

And Democritus drew a sharp distinction, fundamental to his positive ethical and political theory, between the subjectively variable pleasant and the objectively determinable good or true:

> To all humans the same thing is good and true, but different people find different things pleasant. (D/K B69; McK 30)

Several sources report that Democritus was a great stylist, speaking of him in the same breath as Plato. If Galen is to be trusted, Democritus may even have anticipated Plato's development of the dialogue into a full-blown art-form. At least, he seems to have composed a mini-dialogue, an *agon* (contest), pitting Intellect against the Senses. This seems to represent *in nuce* his attempt at an epistemological compromise:

> *Intellect*: Sweet is by convention and bitter by convention, hot by convention, cold by convention, colour by convention; in truth there are but atoms and the void.
> *Senses*: Wretched mind, from us are you taking the evidence by which you would overthrow us? Our overthrow is your own downfall. (D/K B125)

For Democritus, we might say, pure reason, without benefit of sense-perception, was like a potter without hands or clay. On the other hand, sense-impressions, and the images through which they impinge on the mind, can deceive. The way to understanding is to be found in some judicious mixture of intellectual reason and sensory experience. How then does Democritus' quintessential 'atoms and void' doctrine fit in with this epistemology?

That which Democritus, like his fellow devotees of enquiry (*historia*), wished to know or at least understand was *phusis*, the world of nature. The affirmation of 'Intellect' that 'in truth there are but atoms and the void' was Democritus' own considered view. But whether that view should be dubbed materialist, let alone hailed (as by Marx) as the mother and father of all materialisms, is a separate question. The humorous mnemonic 'What is mind? No matter. What is matter? Never mind' may work well as a post-Cartesian binary opposition, but the ancient Greeks saw the world in less clear-cut terms. Their word that we translate 'soul' or 'mind', *psukhê*, was often conceived as having an importantly material component, if not basis, and was indeed taken by Democritus to be entirely material. On the other hand, Democritus did not understand, analyse or gain access to *phusis* through what we could consider properly empirical means. Behind the would-be totalizing 'atoms and the void' definition there lurks an ineradicable quotient of axiomatic and *a priori* stipulation.

The longest account of Democritus' atomism is contained in a report by Simplicius, a late commentator on Aristotle, which purports to be a quotation from Aristotle's essay 'On Democritus':

Democritus thinks that the nature of eternal things

11

consists in small substances, infinite in quantity, and for them he posits a place, distinct from them and infinite in extent. He calls places by the names 'void', 'nothing' and 'infinite'; and each of the substances he calls 'thing', 'solid' and 'being'. He thinks that the substances are so small that they escape our senses, and that they possess all sorts of forms and all sorts of shapes and differences in magnitude. From them, as from elements, he was able to generate and compound visible and perceptible bodies. The atoms struggle and are carried about in the void because of their dissimilarities and the other differences mentioned, and as they are carried about they collide and are bound together in a binding which makes them touch and be contiguous with one another but which does not genuinely produce any other single nature whatever from them; for it is utterly silly to think that two or more things could ever become one. He explains how the substances remain together in terms of the ways in which the bodies entangle with and grasp hold of one another; for some of them are uneven, some hooked, some concave, some convex, and others have innumerable other differences. So he thinks that they hold on to one another and remain together up to the time when some stronger force reaches them from their environment and shakes them and scatters them apart. He speaks of generation and of its contrary, dissolution, not only in connection with animals but also in connection with plants and worlds – and in general with all perceptible bodies. (D/K A37; B pp. 247–8)

Democritus' atoms, it has been remarked, seem on this account somewhat to resemble Lego bricks, in their capacity for recombination to form different entities while consisting of the same fundamental stuff. Yet this passage from Simplicius illustrates (rather than explains) Democritean atomism. Further illustration (and no more) is provided by a passage from Aristotle's extant treatise *Metaphysics* that associates Democritus with the shadowy Leucippus:

> Just as those who make the underlying substance single generate other things by its properties, so these men [Leucippus and Democritus] say that the differences [among the atoms] are the causes of the other things. They say that the differences are three in number – shape, order, and position. For they say that beings differ only by 'rhythm', 'contact' and 'mode' – where rhythm is shape, contact is order and mode is position. The letter A differs from N in shape; AN differs from NA in order; and N differs from Z in position. (D/K A6; B p. 248)

Who – and even whether – Leucippus was, is unclear today, as it seemingly was in antiquity too: Epicurus at any rate denied his very existence, and he was followed in that by at least one major commentator (Sextus Empiricus). More important, however, is why Democritus supposed the world to consist of atoms and void, and nothing but, and that is something which those texts signally fail to reveal. An extract from Aristotle's *On Generation and Corruption* may take us as close to that explanation as we are going to get:

> There is a difficulty if one supposes that there is a body or magnitude which is divisible everywhere and that this division is possible. For what will there be that escapes the division? If it is divisible everywhere, and the division is possible, then it might be so divided at one and the

same time even if the divisions were not all made at the same time; and if this were to happen, no impossibility would result. So if it is by nature everywhere divisible, then if it is divided – whether at successive mid-points or by any other method – nothing impossible will have come about. . . .

Aristotle then continues to exemplify by paradox, not necessarily reproducing Democritus' own arguments but presumably adapting genuine Democritean material (which might itself have been designed to counter in kind the type of paradoxical argumentation dear to the Eleatic Zeno, see below):

Let us assume a body that is divisible throughout, and let us further assume that it has been so divided. What would then be left over? Not a magnitude, clearly, since that could be further divided, but we supposed it divisible everywhere. But if there is to be no body nor magnitude left, and yet the division is to take place, then the body must be composed of points, and its components will have no magnitude, or of nothing at all, so that it would come to be, and be composed, from nothing and the whole body would be nothing but an appearance. . . . But it is absurd to think that a magnitude consists of what are not magnitudes. (D/K A9; B pp. 250–1)

Hence bodies, for Democritus, are not infinitely divisible; and the cosmos must consist of atoms, *a-toma* or 'indivisibles', and not-bodies or void, that is really existent empty space. Aristotle himself, however, was not convinced; for him, bodies were, potentially, infinitely divisible. But not even the weight of Aristotle's authority was found universally compelling. Most significantly, his younger contemporary Epicurus reaffirmed atomism in the later fourth and early third century BC, on grounds of explanatory economy, though the anti-teleological Epicurus probably also found Democritus' resolutely materialist atomism congenial for other than purely 'scientific' reasons.

Why, then, did it so greatly matter to Democritus that atomism should be right, should fulfil its explanatory tasks? On the one hand, negatively, because of what, or whom, he was arguing against. This was chiefly the steady-state-universe school of the Eleatics (named after their base at Greek Elea in south Italy), Parmenides and Zeno, and their eastern Greek follower, Melissus of Samos. These conservative thinkers eliminated generation and destruction from their worldview, since those processes involved, inadmissibly in their opinion, prior and posterior states of nothingness, and they claimed that what was, was so eternally, unchangeably. The static implications of their material philosophy for social and political theory appealed enormously to Plato, who applied Eleatic criteria to moral concepts, thereby producing his perfect, unchanging Forms, which were in turn the basis for objectively grounded ethical truths. Democritus accepted the Eleatics' postulate of eternity – nothing can come from nothing; but he decisively rejected their postulate of stasis: with Heraclitus, an Ionian predecessor from Ephesus (floruit c. 500 BC), he believed that everything was, on the contrary, in flux.

On the other hand, Democritus' atoms helped him positively to explain, to his own satisfaction at least, many other puzzles, not least the nature of the universe itself.

COSMOLOGY AND COSMOGRAPHY[8]

The ancient Greek word *kosmos*, from which we derive our 'cosmos', meant originally order, orderly arrangement, as applied to such mundane realities as – to take a standard Homeric example – the order of battle. By Democritus' day it had acquired the modern sense that we unconsciously borrow. This extension of meaning seemed entirely apt, since the cosmos was generally assumed by Greeks to be a universe both orderly and (in a strong, active sense) ordered. Compare and, more significantly, contrast Democritus.

Among his many works listed by Thrasylus are the *Little World-System*, the *Cosmography* and *On the Planets*, said to be works of natural science. Other relevant titles not integrated into Thrasylus' catalogue include: *Heavenly Causes, Atmospheric Causes, Terrestrial Causes, Causes Concerned with Fire and Things in Fire*. And among his 'mathematical' works was a *Description of the Heavens*. From these somehow descend the fragments we have, including this one (from Diogenes Laertius):

> Leucippus [standing here for 'Leucippus-and-Democritus'] holds that the whole is infinite ... part of it is full and part void. . . . Hence arise infinite worlds, and hence these are resolved again into these elements. The worlds come into being as follows: many bodies of all sorts of shapes move 'by abscission from the infinite' into a great void; they come together there and produce a single whirl (or vortex, *dinê*) in which, colliding with one another and revolving in all sorts of ways, they begin to separate apart, like to like.

16

But when their multitude prevents them from rotating any longer in equilibrium, those that are fine go out towards the surrounding void as if sifted, while the rest 'abide together' and, becoming entangled, unite their motions and make a first spherical structure.

This structure stands apart like a 'membrane' which contains in itself all kinds of bodies; and as they whirl around owing to the resistance of the middle, the surrounding membrane becomes thin, while contiguous atoms keep flowing together owing to contact with the whirl. So the earth came into being, the atoms that had been borne to the middle abiding together there. Again, the containing membrane is itself increased, owing to the attraction of bodies outside. As it moves around in the whirl it takes in anything it touches. Some of these bodies that get entangled form a structure that is at first moist and muddy, but as they revolve with the whirl of the whole they dry out and then ignite to form the substance of the heavenly bodies. (D/K A1; K/R/S 563)

One of the most important issues at stake in what has been considered a cosmological crisis or at least crux in classical antiquity was whether the cosmos was infinite. All parties accepted the view that the region we inhabit and perceive was a closed world. But, in contrast to the view later espoused most authoritatively by Plato and Aristotle, Democritus postulated beyond our closed world the existence of void space and matter that formed itself into other, infinite worlds. Opinions differ as to what prompted Democritus into conceiving the universe to be infinite, but one modern suggestion (Furley's) is that without that postulate he could not have explained the dual motions of the cosmos, circular and rectilinear, in accordance with his own atomist principles.

The empirical status, or basis, of this account is no less tenuous, though at any rate the 'like to like' behaviour of atoms is presumably connected to the traditional 'like to like' rule of the behaviour of things, both animate and inanimate, that Democritus elsewhere elaborates as follows (the reference to the 'whirling of the sieve' is suggestive):

> Animals, he says, congregate with animals of the same kind – doves with doves, cranes with cranes, and so with the other irrational animals. Similarly in the case of inanimate things, as we can see from seeds in a sieve and from pebbles on the sea-shore. For in the one case the whirling of the sieve separately arranges lentils with lentils, barley with barley, wheat with wheat; and in the other case, by the motion of the waves, oval pebbles are forced into the same place as oval pebbles, and round pebbles as round pebbles, as though the similarity in things contained some sort of force for collecting things together. (D/K B264; B p. 249)

Nor is it quite clear how the formation of worlds is supposed on Democritean principles to occur. The above account seems to envisage a two-stages theory: first, within a large patch of void a large collection of atoms becomes isolated; second, the collection of atoms thus formed in turn forms a whirl or vortex (*dinê*). But how precisely this is supposed to happen is not further specified, other than in general theoretical terms of 'necessity':

> Everything happens according to necessity; for the cause of coming-into-being of all things is the whirl (vortex), which he [Democritus] calls necessity. (Diog. Laert. 9.45; K/R/S 566)

other's ways. The sounds of their voices were confused and unintelligible at first, but gradually they articulated words, and by establishing signs (*symbola*) for each existing thing, they taught each other the meanings of them. But since communities of this sort emerged throughout the inhabited world, people did not all have the same language, since each community assigned expressions to things by chance. This is why there are all different kinds of languages today; moreover, from these original communities come all the different peoples.

The first human beings lived lives full of hardship, since none of the things we use in our lives had yet been discovered: they had no clothing, knew nothing of housing or fire, and were entirely ignorant of agriculture. Since they did not know about the harvesting of wild food, they did not store up any produce for times of need. As a result, many of them died during the winters because of the cold and lack of food; but from this they gradually learned by experience how to take refuge in caves in the winter and how to store up those fruits that could be kept. And when they had come to know fire and the other useful things, gradually they also learned crafts and the other things that can benefit the life of the community. For as a general rule in all things need itself was people's teacher, providing the appropriate instruction in each area for a creature that was both well endowed by nature and had helpers for everything, namely hands and language and a shrewd mind. (D/K 5; G/W 1)

That passage is taken from a cosmogony, zoogony and anthropology contained in a historical compendium of world history compiled in the first century BC by a Sicilian

Greek, Diodorus, who was himself drawing on the third-century treatise *On the Egyptians* by Hecataeus of Abdera. Democritus is not cited by name as its author or part-author, and there are some non-Democritean features in the cosmogony and zoogony. But the anthropology does arguably bear the stamp of Democritus' thinking, especially the distinctive emphasis on necessity as the mother of social invention. It is also consistent with an odd group of four Democritean fragments, collected in Stobaeus' chapter 'On Laws and Customs':

> Concerning the slaughter or non-slaughter of certain animals, the rule is as follows: he who kills those which do or are disposed to do harm suffers no penalty, and to do so shall be for well-being rather than otherwise.

> It is needful to kill those creatures which do damage contrary to right, all of them at all costs. And he who does this shall have a greater share of good cheer, of justice, of security and of property in every social order.

> As has been written about enemies in the form of foxes and reptiles, so too it seems to me necessary to act in the case of men: in accordance with ancestral laws, in every social order in which law does not debar it. (In fact, it is prohibited by religious sanctuaries in each country, and by treaties and oaths.)

> Anyone killing a brigand or pirate should go unpunished, whether he does so by his own hand, by issuing an order, or by voting. (D/K B257–260; P pp. 23–7)

The underlying message here seems to be that men, having existed originally in isolated groups at the mercy of wild animals, found themselves compelled to live together in cities for their own self-protection and obliged, once thus 'civilized', to enforce the laws rigorously against both human and non-human threats, subject only to the constraints of ultimately religious prohibitions. It is instructive to compare and contrast this necessitarian but optimistic approach to human sociopolitical origins and development with some other Greek speculative writings.

For example, in the Diodoran scheme there is no aboriginal (divinely blest) golden age from which the contemporary (accursedly human) iron age marks the lowest point of declension, such as we find in Hesiod's authoritative hexameter poem *Works and Days* (*c.* 700 BC). Nor is the present state of mankind considered so awful that the desired human condition of the future is figured as a state of automatic utopia, with the necessities of life being constantly available on tap without the application of human labour, such as we find it described wishfully in contemporary fifth-century Athenian comedies. Instead, what we have is an idea of controlled progress from an undesirably brutish past towards a really quite acceptable present. This may be considered congenial to modern ways of thinking, but in its ancient context it was really quite eccentric.

It was not altogether out on a limb, however. In the stress on the benefits of language and craft-inventiveness, for example, there is a distinct affinity between our putatively Democritean passage and the famous 'Ode to Man' in Sophocles' tragedy *Antigone* (originally staged probably in 441 BC):

Numberless wonders
terrible wonders walk the world but none the match for
    man …

23

> He conquers all ...
> And speech and thought, quick as the wind
> and the mood and mind for law that rules the city –
> all these he has taught himself. [trs. Robert Fagles]

The Ode goes on to draw moral and political implications from human inventiveness, in a manner somewhat recalling the myth of origins put in the mouth of Democritus' fellow-Abderite Protagoras by Plato in the dialogue *Protagoras*. The lesson of that myth was that *dikê* (justice) and *aidôs* (shame), essential preconditions for civilized political life, were common human characteristics granted to mankind by Zeus. No such lesson is drawn in our passage; a secularized version of that myth is, however, to be found in the author known as the 'Anonymus Iamblichi', who has quite plausibly been identified with Democritus:

> if humans were by nature incapable of living alone and thus joined together, yielding to necessity, and have developed their whole way of life and the skills required for this end, and cannot be with each other while living in a condition of lawlessness – because of all these constraints law and justice are king among us and will never be displaced, for their strength is engrained in our nature. (G/W p. 293)

For the 'Anonymus Iamblichi', therefore, human nature is partly a matter of learning from experience – as it is for Democritus in writings more certainly attributable to him. Indeed, Democritus goes further, in claiming apparently that in a sense a person makes him or herself:

> Nature and teaching are closely related; for teaching reforms a person, and by reforming remakes his nature. (D/K B33; G/W 33)

We shall return to that – contentious – contention in the context of Democritus' own ethical and political teachings.

PSYCHOLOGY AND MEDICINE[11]

In the ancient Greek city, unlike our own Western polities, the principle of the separation of the powers of government (legislative, executive, judicial) was but dimly apprehended and applied very loosely if at all. It came naturally therefore to ordinary Greeks, especially those living in a democratic city or aspiring to do so, to envisage practical politics in terms not just of voting in elections but of legislation and litigation, including litigation that we would consider private rather than public. From that second-nature identification arose one of Democritus' most striking metaphors:

> Lay down this law for your soul: do not do anything improper. (from D/K B264; G/W 29)

No less arresting is Democritus' legalistic personification of the mind–body relationship:

> If the body were to take the soul to court for the pains and suffering it had endured throughout its life, then if he were to be on the jury for the case he would gladly cast his vote against the soul inasmuch as it had destroyed some parts of the body by negligence or dissipated them by drunkenness, and had ruined and ravaged other parts by its pursuit of pleasures – just as he would blame the careless user if a tool or utensil were in a bad condition. (D/K B259; B p. 264)

The soul (*psukhê*) to which these passages are addressed

must not be confused with our conception of an immaterial, spiritual essence. In other Greek writers, *psukhê* according to context may mean mind or intellect, sexual passion, courage or simply life, as well as soul. In Democritus, it was, *ex hypothesi*, no less material than the body, throughout which indeed soul-atoms were held to be distributed. The body, moreover, which Democritus graphically refers to as a 'tent' (*skênos*, D/K B223), was the soul's natural habitation, not (as other thinkers conceived) its tomb, prison or place of exile. Democritus' soul is the cause of life and sensation. It is composed of fine round atoms and forms a compound no less perishable than the body. Perception occurs as a result of the impact on the soul-atoms, through the organs of sensation, of *eidola*, that is thin atomic membranes shed from the surface of sensible objects. Qualities that may be perceived – taste, colour, and so on – are the product of the combination of the atoms of the sensible object and those of the perceiving soul.

A fairly full account of Democritean perception-theory is preserved in a work of Theophrastus, Aristotle's pupil (and successor as head of the Lyceum institute he had founded in the mid-330s), the *On the Senses*; here are just a couple of extracts, the first regarding sight:

He attempts to account for each of the senses in turn. He has sight occur by reflection, but he talks of reflection in a special way. The reflection does not take place immediately in the pupil; rather, the air between the eye and the seen object is imprinted when it is compressed by what is seen and what sees (for there are always effluences coming off everything). Then this air, which is solid and has a different colour, is reflected in the eyes, which are moist. What is dense does not receive it, but what is moist lets it pass through. That is why moist eyes are better at seeing than hard eyes – provided that the external integument is extremely fine and dense, the internal parts are as spongy as possible and empty of any dense and strong flesh and also of any thick and oily liquid, and the vessels leading to the eyes are straight and dry so as to take the same shape as the objects imprinted – for each thing best recognizes what is akin to it.

Then, with respect to taste:

Flavours are *sharp* if their shapes [determined by their constituent atoms – PC] are angular and crinkled and small and fine. For because of their asperity they quickly pass through everywhere, and being rough and angular they gather and hold things together. That is why they heat the body, by making emptiness in it – for what is most empty is most easily heated.

Sweet flavour is constituted by round shapes which are not too small. That is why they relax the body completely without doing so violently or passing through all of it quickly. They disturb the other shapes because as they pass through they make the others drift about and they moisten them; and when these are moistened and move out of order, they flow together into the stomach – that is the most accessible part, since it is the emptiest. *Sour* flavour is constituted by large shapes with many angles and as little roundness as possible. For when these enter the body they clog and stop the vessels and prevent the shapes from flowing together. That is why they also settle the bowels. *Bitter* flavour is constituted by small, smooth, rounded shapes, where the roundness also contains crinkles. That is why it is viscous and sticky. *Salty* flavour is constituted by large shapes which are not rounded – ‹nor yet uneven but angular and crinkled› – he calls uneven those which entangle and interwine with one another. They are large, because salt rises to the surface – if they were small and were struck by the shapes around them, they would mix with the whole. They are not round, because what is salty is rough whereas what is rounded is smooth. They are not uneven, because they do not tangle themselves one with another – that is why it is friable. *Pungent* flavour is small, rounded and angular, but not uneven. For the pungent, being angular, heats by its roughness, and it relaxes because it is small and rounded and angular. For that is what the angular is like.

And so, finally, on to perception in general, ending on a typically relativistic note:

> He treats the other powers of each thing in the same way, reducing them to the shapes. Of all the shapes none is pure and unmixed with any others, but there are many in each – the same flavour contains smooth and rough, rounded and sharp, and the rest. The shape which preponderates has a very great influence with regard to our perception and its own effect – so too has the condition in which it finds us. For this too makes no little difference, since sometimes the same thing has opposite effects and opposites the same effect. (B pp. 257–9)

The soul–body distinction was mirrored within the soul itself by the distinction and opposition of a ratiocinative, intellectual component and an emotive or appetitive component, the former being regularly privileged above the latter by idealistic self-denying intellectuals and philosophers such as Democritus. There is perhaps a hint of puritanism at work here, or at any rate a determined emphasis on stringent moderation and self-control:

> All those who make their pleasures from the belly, exceeding the right time [or measure] for food, drink, or sex, have short-lived pleasures – only for as long as they eat or drink – but many pains. (D/K B235; C/M 32)

The notion of a right time or measure (*kairos*) was popular among the medical writers, from whom Democritus was perhaps borrowing here. It was later emphasized by, for example, the Democritean thinker Anaxarchus, who accompanied Alexander the Great on his prodigious expedition of conquest throughout the Middle East. Medicine, 'scientific' medicine, was indeed one of the most conspicuous intellectual achievements of Democritus' generation and lifetime, and one with which Democritus was in full sympathy. It is a sad loss therefore that we do not have his *Prognosis*, *On Diet* or *Dietetics*, *Medical Judgement* and *On Fever and Coughing Sicknesses*.

The standard, 'popular' view of disease regarded it as literally god-sent – thus, to take a famous instance, had Homer represented the pestilence afflicting the Greeks at Troy at the very beginning of the *Iliad*. Even the ultra-rationalist Pericles was made by Thucydides to refer to the plague that devastated Athens in 430 as something *daimonion*, demonic, of more than natural, that is human, causation and explanation. But perhaps that was playing to the gallery in a speech delivered before the Athenian democratic assembly. In sharp contrast, the contemporary author of a written tract 'On the Sacred Disease' vigorously denied that the terrifying illness of epilepsy was any more sacred than any other disease, since all diseases were equally 'sacred' and equally susceptible of naturalistic analysis and explanation; and he roundly denounced the quacks who made a tidy living through trading on such irrational fears.

That fearless writer was a member of the medical school founded on the east Aegean island of Cos by Hippocrates, who was perhaps an almost exact coeval of Democritus. It was in the same 'Hippocratic' spirit that Democritus himself is said to have opined:

> if you open yourself up, within you you will find a large and varied storehouse and treasury of ills, which do not flow in from outside but have, as it were, internal and native springs. (D/K B149; B p. 264)

For these ills, the cure he advocated was medicine, rational medicine, which:

> cures the diseases of the body, [as] wisdom clears the soul of passions. (B p. 265)

Precisely the wrong way of going about – and thinking about – healthcare, according to Democritus, was to apply for relief to the gods:

> Men ask for health in their prayers to the gods: they do not realize that the power to achieve it lies in themselves. Lacking self-control, they perform contrary actions and betray health to their desires. (D/K B234; B p. 275)

From physical health to mental and moral health was therefore for Democritus but a short step. The goal of the ethical cleansing of the individual soul could be described conventionally as happiness (*eudaimoniê* – though that equally conventional translation disguises the element of luck and the connotation of worldly success conveyed by the Greek term) or, more specifically, as cheerfulness (*euthumiê* – see next section). As Clement of Alexandria put it, 'Democritus and Plato both place happiness in the soul' (D/K B170; B p. 265), and perhaps Democritus himself wrote something like:

> Happiness does not dwell in herds, nor yet in gold: the soul is the dwelling place of a man's lot. (D/K B171; B p. 265)

That may seem to foreshadow the notion first fully excogitated by Plato, that one's *daimôn* or lot, one's self as we might say, was to be located in the soul or personality. Yet Democritus on the evidence available does not pursue the corollary of that placement, that is, the revolutionary thrust developed by Socratic–Platonic moral philosophy away from the primary concern for public life and the public good and towards an overriding preoccupation with the moral health of the individual and especially the preternaturally gifted soul.

Democritus' concern, an unusually pronounced one, is rather with what we would call conscience:

> Even when you are alone, neither say nor do anything bad: learn to feel shame before yourself rather than before others. (D/K B144; B p. 275)

This has indeed been hailed as probably the most original feature of his ethical doctrine, since it subverts the traditional, that is public, shame standard of Greek morality. Yet the premise and motivation of that injunction of self-awareness and self-policing are that a good conscience will not only be more pleasurable than a bad one, individually and personally speaking, but also lead to better relationships with and behaviour towards others, in and for the good of society. That was no doubt somewhat utopian, but it was all of a piece with his broadly communitarian ethical and political theory.

ETHICS AND POLITICS[12]

Of the sixty works attributed to Democritus in the ancient catalogue compiled by Thrasylus (*Prolegomena to the Reading of the Books of Democritus*) just eight were classified as 'ethical': *Pythagoras, On the Disposition of the Wise Man, On the Things in Hades, Tritogeneia, On Manliness* or *On Virtue, The Horn of Amaltheia, On Contentment* and *Ethical Commentaries*. Yet over four-fifths of the extant, allegedly verbatim fragments are concerned with ethics. Of course size is not everything. But my hunch is that the plurality of preserved ethical fragments does not altogether misrepresent the importance Democritus himself attached to his ethical writings, or – would it be more accurate to say? – to his ethical-cum-political writings. In ancient Greece generally, and more specifically within the framework of the ancient Greek polis or city, being a good person and being a good citizen were normally, and normatively, taken as pretty much the same thing. How far was Democritus a subscriber to this conventional view?

The ancient Greek citizen, in the full, active and participatory sense, was always by definition an adult male. Women need not apply. And that Democritus was deeply concerned with promoting the good civic life for men in the gender sense may probably be inferred from his robustly, but not alas untypically, chauvinist view of the civic capacity of women:

> To be ruled by a woman would be the ultimate insult (*hubris*) to a man. (D/K B111; B. G/W 19)

The precise connotation of *hubris* here is that of the transgression or violation of status-boundaries, issuing from the 'naturalistic' premise or rather dogma that it was Man's nature to rule naturally inferior Woman. Yet in actual historical fact, as Democritus observes with feeling:

> Some men rule cities and are slaves to women. (D/K B214; B p. 271)

That state of affairs was doubly transgressive, since male citizens were 'naturally' free, not slaves or slavish, as well as superordinate. Democritus' observation here anticipates, and may have the same source of inspiration as, Aristotle's critique of Sparta in the second book of the *Politics*. Gynaecocracy (the rule of women over men) was in Aristotle's similarly prejudiced view characteristic of military societies like Sparta, which Aristotle criticized sharply on this and other important counts. The overall attitude of Democritus to Sparta is not known, though one would guess (from his democratic sympathies, see below) that it was not altogether favourable. His anti-feminism, on the other hand, was so palpable that it even led him into attempting to foreclose to women the sphere of activity by which classical Greek culture is sometimes plausibly hailed as an age of enlightenment:

> Do not let a woman practise reasoned argument (*logos*); that is frightful. (D/K B110; G/W 20)

Whereas 'Reason', when practised by a male citizen presumably, 'is a powerful persuader' (B p. 265), and all the more admirable for that, Democritus seems to have shared the view espoused by many suffering males in Athenian tragedy that in the mouth of a woman *logos* was poison.

Democritus was not by any means alone among Greek political philosophers in privileging men above women. Only Plato, to a limited extent, swam against that tide, provoking thereby a torrent of counter-argument from his most distinguished pupil (especially in the first book of the *Politics*). Consistently, therefore, Democritus privileged the male, public space of the city above the private, domestic sphere, providing us into the bargain with the earliest known attestation of a phrase that is to be a keynote of both Plato's and Aristotle's political philosophy:

Learn the political craft (*politike techné*), since it is the greatest, and pursue its labours, which lead to great and glorious things. (D/K B157; G/W 6)

However, Democritus' scanting of the domestic domain took a particularly sharp and unconventional form, by its diminishing of the normally recognized and honoured biological function of male citizens' wives as producers of the next generation of citizens:

The possession of children seems to be a necessity for humans, supported by nature and long-established custom. (D/K B278; G/W 34)

But:

Whoever feels a need to have children does better, I think, to get them from friends [by adoption]. C D/K B277; G/W 35)

That unusual recommendation may perhaps be connected with his apparent downgrading of the sexual act itself, though this might rather be part of what I have called his 'puritanism' towards physical pleasures in general:

> Men enjoy scratching themselves – they get the same
> pleasure as those who are having sexual intercourse.
> (D/K B127; B p. 264)

At all events, however they were acquired, children had
to be formally educated, though he insisted that that could
and should be achieved reasonably cheaply:

> It is possible to educate your children without spending
> much of your money, and thus to erect a protective wall
> around their persons and property. (D/K B280; G/W 37)

The aim of education, however, might on occasion be not
merely conservative, to ensure the solid transmission of a
society's received values, but radical individual transforma-
tion:

> Nature and teaching are closely related; for teaching
> reforms a person, and by reforming remakes his nature.
> (D/K B33; G/W 33)

Once thus educated to understand his natural capacity, a
citizen was again recommended the way of moderation:

> Whoever wishes to be content in life should not engage
> in many activities, either public or private, nor do
> anything beyond his ability and nature. (D/K B3; G/W
> 31)

There may be an undertone there of the oligarchs' favourite
critique of democratic 'busybodying' (*polupragmosunê*), but
if so it is muted. For moderation was encouraged by
Democritus not only in deeds but also in possessions:

> he should protect himself so that when fortune strikes ...
> he can put it aside. For a moderate amount is more
> secure than a large amount. (D/K B3; G/W 31)

Wealth and poverty were intimately connected, in Greek thought and practice, with the form of a city's political constitution. Aristotle was merely being extremely explicit when in the *Pollitics* he concluded bluntly that democracy was the rule of the poor, and oligarchy (literally 'rule of the few') the rule of the rich, even if the rich should – *per impossibile* – make up the majority of a state's citizen body. Hence arose Democritus' automatic linkage of poverty with democracy, since etymologically that form of government represented the sovereign power (*kratos*) of the *demos* or People, and pragmatically, in accordance with Aristotle's realistic sociology of Greek politics, the rule of the 'poor' majority of the citizenry:

> Poverty in a democracy is preferable to so-called prosperity among dictators (*dunastai*) to the same extent as freedom is to slavery. (D/K B251; P p. 27)

Freedom, personal independence and poverty were thus for Democritus compatible. Yet his was not a widespread let alone the normative view, since possession of wealth typically brought with it political power, and that power might as easily be exercised over a poor fellow-citizen as over a stranger or slave (or wife and children). Indeed, the power of the rich over the poor citizens was regularly equated with 'slavery' on the part of the powerless or disempowered.

Underpinning the exercise of political power in a Greek city was an elaborately coded moral vocabulary, ultimately aristocratic in origin. A 'good' man or a 'sensible' man was automatically assumed to be a rich (and often also aristocratic) man, a 'bad' man conversely a poor one. But Democritus, true to form, unconventionally drove a wedge between these time-hallowed identifications:

> A sensible person bears poverty well. (D/K B291; G/W
> 11)

> Poverty, wealth: these are names for need and suffi-
> ciency. Someone in need is not wealthy; someone
> without need is not poor. (D/K B283; G/W 9)

A middling condition, therefore, in which one's needs and
desires were kept in a moderate and stable balance by
intelligent self-understanding and self-control, that would
seem to be the Democritean ideal. Enough was as good as a
feast.

Again, so far as governance was concerned, office-holders
in a Greek city, whether democratic or oligarchic, tended to
be rich men – wealth being a necessary condition of the
leisure required for devotion to a career in politics. Office-
holders were therefore in conventional Greek moral–political terms 'good' men. But Democritus was crucially keen
and able to distinguish between their socio-economic status
and their moral worth:

> By nature ruling belongs to the superior (D/K B267;
> G/W 2)

a general maxim in which the Greek word translated
'superior' (*kreissones*) could mean either morally better or
politically or just physically stronger, but:

> When bad men (*kakoi*) gain office, the more unworthy
> they are on entry, the more they become thoughtless
> and full of folly and recklessness, (D/K B254; G/W 16)

and:

> There is no device in the present shape of society to stop
> the wrongdoing of officials, however thoroughly good

they may be. ... (D/K B266; P p. 30)

'Good' men (as the world saw them) could therefore be 'bad' men (as Democritus saw them). Democritus was thus capable of questioning the aristocrats' or oligarchs' claim to rule on grounds of their innate superior fitness. No less un- or anti-aristocratic was his emphasis on the need for sheer hard grind (*ponoi*) on the part of those engaged in public life. But did these attitudes make him, if only by implication, an ideological democrat?

That case has been advanced in recent scholarship, with subtlety and cogency. Yet the fragments we have, though compatible with such a view, do not enforce the inference. What they prove, rather, is Democritus' pre-eminent concern for political security and stability:

> Factional strife (*stasis*) within the group is bad for both sides, for it destroys the victors and the vanquished alike. (D/K B249; G/W 5)

> With concord (*homonoia*) cities are able to accomplish the greatest deeds in war, but not otherwise. (D/K B250; G/W 4)

> To affairs of state one should, above all else, attach the greatest importance, neither engaging in contentions beyond what is reasonable nor appropriating personal power beyond the common good. For the well-managed polis is the greatest source of success, and all depends on this. If this is saved, all is saved; but if this is destroyed, then all is destroyed. (D/K B252; P p. 23)

That paramount preoccupation of his was no doubt under-girded by close experience of the disease of *stasis* (civil discord or strife, even outright civil war) between polarized factions of self-styled democrats and oligarchs, such as was so memorably described and diagnosed in book 3 of Thucydides' contemporary *History of the Peloponnesian War* (fought by Athens and Sparta and their respective allies from 431 to 404 BC). How, then, could and should *homonoia*, literally 'same-mindedness', be secured and maintained? One powerful Democritean answer was, by a prophylactic redistribution of wealth from rich citizens to poor:

> When those in power venture to provide funds for the poor and to do them services and be kind to them, the result is compassion, an end to isolation, the formation of comradeships, mutual assistance and concord among the citizens, and other benefits too numerous to list. (D/K B255; G/W 12)

But was this redistribution to be the outcome of old-style paternalism, the aristocratic–oligarchic approach to politics, or of a legally binding obligation imposed on the rich, according to the democratic method of liturgy-payment as practised in classical Athens (a *leitourgia*, such as the financing of the chorus of a tragedy or comedy, was literally a work performed for the people)? Democritus does not say. Nor, vitally, do we have evidence pertaining to Democritus' conception of and attitude to political equality (*isonomia politikê*). So we cannot claim, without reservation, that Democritus was a radical Periclean democrat, as opposed to, say, an unusually liberal-minded oligarch. It would also be unwarranted, tempting though it may be, to explain Plato's silence about Democritus on the grounds that he knew – and despised – the Abderite's democratic political outlook.

Perhaps, rather, since Democritus certainly shared many

qualities of thought and expression with Thucydides,[13] he shared too the revisionist Athenian historian's strikingly advanced preference for a 'mixed' form of constitution, neither democratic nor oligarchic, that would somehow provide adequate political power, privilege and recognition for both the few rich and the poor many. That mixture Thucydides called a *krasis*, which is the Athenian form of Democritus' own word, *krêsis*, for the desirable self-regulating balance or 'dynamic equilibrium' (Vlastos) that characterized a healthy state of soul.

We have left the big issue to the last. If push came to shove, would Democritus have been prepared to sacrifice involvement in the public life of politics, often enough a pretty dirty game, for the sake of keeping his soul healthy and clean? Put that question another way: are all those fragments which assert or imply a commitment to public virtue, to promoting the good of the political community as a whole, to be regarded as trumped by those fragments which focus on the need to secure and maintain the best possible condition of one's individual soul?

Perhaps surprisingly, it may be Diogenes Laertius (9.45) who of all ancient writers captured most accurately the essence of his biographical subject's broadly ethical philosophy:

> The goal or summation (*telos*) is *euthumia*, though this is not the same as pleasure (as some have mistakenly understood it to be by tradition and hearsay), but is the state according to which the soul is in a calm and well-balanced condition, disturbed by no fear, superstition or any other emotion. Another of the many names he uses for it is *euestô* (well-being).

The use of *telos* is strictly anachronistic, but Democritus' best-known ethical work was indeed the *Peri Euthumiês* – or 'On Cheerfulness', to which he gave a characteristically moderate spin:

> Cheerfulness arises in people through moderation of enjoyment and due proportion in life. Deficiencies and excesses tend to change suddenly and give rise to large movements in the soul. (D/K B191; C/M 28)

Does that mean that in order to avoid such destabilizing and debilitating soul-motions the ideal Democritean should, other things being equal, seek the quiet life away from the public political arena? I am confident it does not, and the clue to the correct interpretation lies I would argue in the good Ionian word *euestô* or 'well-being'.

It would be characteristic of Democritus' worldly as well as this-worldly moral philosophizing if that word was intended to refer to the possession of material rather than spiritual goods, to (of course) the 'necessary', that is right and proper, degree. Democritus was no solipsist, for all his unusual attentiveness to respect for oneself as well as for others, and despite his emphasis on self-generated, internally motivated virtues. Merely having a good soul without exercising its virtues where they should be exercised, in public for the common good, would have been for him and the fairly elevated level of society he was addressing in his writings a largely pointless exercise. Even Plato, after all, in the *Republic* required his true philosophers, those who had seen the Light and understood the Form of the Good, to go back down into the Cave (the benighted real world of everyday political life) so as to illuminate it with their uniquely privileged insight. It would be odd therefore if the far less metaphysically minded Democritus had adopted a more disengaged stance than Plato on both the ethics of (political) practice and the practice of (political) ethics. To repeat, in conclusion:

> the well-managed polis is the greatest source of success, and all depends on this. If this is saved, all is saved; but if this is destroyed, then all is destroyed. (D/K B252; P p. 23)

RECEPTION: DEMOCRITUS' LAST LAUGH

Plato was, we have noted, ringingly silent about Democritus by name, but other fourth-century Greek luminaries were not. It is chiefly thanks to Aristotle, if often through his pupils and his commentators, that we have some more than rudimentary idea of Democritus' physics, his equation of the sensible cosmos with 'atoms and the void'. Yet Aristotle was not a Democritean atomist, and he argued against Democritus for a single, finite and eternal cosmos, and for teleological causes. It was probably also against Democritus' ethical writings and his claims for the efficacy of reasoned pedagogy that Aristotle directed his scathing put-down, at the end of his *Nicomachean Ethics*, to the effect that 'discourses on their own ... are powerless to incite the majority of mankind to moral excellence', since the latter are naturally addicted to pleasure-seeking and incapable of being morally transformed by rational argument. Scarcely less hostile, if on other grounds, were the Stoics. On the other hand, Epicurus, who encountered atomism through his teacher Nausiphanes, and Epicurus' poetic Roman follower Lucretius both found the theology and ethics of Democritus profoundly congenial. In Democritus' idea that soul-atoms should be protected from violent upheavals, for example, there is clearly detectable the ancestry of Epicurus' own practical philosophical goal of *ataraxia*, a blissful undisturbedness.

The other side of Democritus' pain-avoidance strategy was a positive encouragement towards cheerfulness, and it is this cheery and cheering aspect of Democritus' thought that features most strongly in his Hellenistic, Roman and later reception. It was perhaps adepts of devil-take-the-hindmost Cynicism who first collected the sententious maxims (*gnômai*, *hupothêkai*) handed down under his name in later antiquity, possibly working from a collection of maxims circulated by Democritus himself. By the time of Horace (died 8 BC) at the latest he had acquired the tag 'the laughing philosopher', and it was as such, rather than for his scientific endeavours, that he was most hymned in the Renaissance and early modern periods. (The first mention of him since antiquity was, however, in Girolamo Fracastoro's *De sympathia et antipathia* of 1545, and the alchemists' reception of him was an indispensable link between ancient natural philosophy and early modern experimental natural science.)

For Montaigne, for example, Democritus was 'a great and famous philosopher', to whom, following the lead of Cicero, he devoted an entire essay 'On Democritus and Heraclitus'. The nub of Montaigne's comparison between the Abderite and his riddling Ephesian predecessor was expressed as follows:

> Democritus and Heraclitus were both philosophers; the former, finding our human circumstances so vain and ridiculous [a Montaigne *avant la lettre*], never went out without a laughing or mocking look on his face: Heraclitus, feeling pity and compassion for these same circumstances of ours, wore an expression which was always sad, his eyes full of tears.[14]

It is as the laughing philosopher that the Spaniard Jusepe de Ribera so memorably captured him *c.* 1635–7 in a painting now hanging in Wilton House.[15]

Today, following the lead given by Karl Marx (whose

doctoral thesis, published only in 1928, pursued a scholarly comparison of the materialist philosophies of Democritus and Epicurus), perception and reception of Democritus are no doubt more sober, if no less appreciative. A university is named after him in northern Greece, as is the prestigious national physics research laboratory in Athens. An international congress has been devoted to his philosophy; so too a spate of important books and papers.[16] If small may be compared with great, he is featured prominently in the bestselling young person's guide to Western philosophy, *Sophie's World*, by Jostein Gaarder, and, more unexpectedly, in Terry Pratchett's 'Discworld' series novel *Small Gods*, besides his appearance, already mentioned, in Gore Vidal's *Creation*.

Perhaps, even so, the state of preservation of his writings, if nothing else, will always prevent his achieving the currency and fame accorded lately to Epicurus (whose *Letter to Menoeceus* has sold over a million copies in an Italian translation). This is greatly to be regretted. For on account of his devotion to reasoned moderation, his unblinking concern to apply a scientific understanding to the worlds of non-human nature and of mankind, and, not least, his unremitting cheerfulness Democritus surely qualifies as a Great Philosopher both in the modern sense and in the enlarged ancient understanding of the term. If philosophical originality consists not only and not so much in novelty, but rather in powerful generalization and the fruitful interrelation of ideas, then Democritus must also be considered one of the most original of the great philosophers.

I draw to a close with my own favourite Democritean passage, taken from the longest ethical fragment in the collection preserved in John Stobaeus' *Anthology*:

You must set your judgement on the possible and be satisfied with what you have, giving little thought to things that are envied and admired, and not dwelling on them in your mind; and you must observe the lives of those who are badly off, considering what they suffer, so that what you have and what belongs to you may seem great and enviable, and, by no longer desiring more, you may not suffer in your soul. For one who admires those who possess much and are deemed blessed by other men and who dwells on them every hour in his memory is compelled always to plan something new and, because of his desire, to set himself to do some pernicious deed that the laws forbid. That is why you must not seek certain things and must be content with others, comparing your own life with that of those who do worse and deeming yourself fortunate, when you reflect on what they undergo, in faring and living so much better than they do. For if you hold fast to this judgement you will live in greater contentment and will drive away those not inconsiderable plagues of life, jealousy and envy and ill-will. (D/K B191; B p. 269)

By re-evaluating the categories according to which we normally reckon success and failure, misery and happiness, Democritus here contends, we shall be led to a more accurate view of our own condition and put ourselves in a position to make positive progress towards what is truly to be desired. Who could say fairer (in both senses), or indeed be more revolutionary (in at least one sense), than that?

It seems only right, though, to leave to the humane and considerate Democritus the last word, on – appropriately – last things. It is a typically cautionary word, redolent also of the Greek intellectual's contempt for unscientific and therefore socially harmful myth. It is a last word, moreover, which certainly unites, as by no means all his attributable writings do, his ethics with his physics, on the ground that a mortal's death, entailing the dissolution of that particular unique conjunction of soul-atoms and body-atoms, is annihilation:

> Some men who do not know how mortal nature dissolves but are aware of the wretchedness of life toil out their lifespan amid upheavals and fears, forging false tales about the time after death. (D/K B297; B p. 284)

NOTES

A Brief Life and Times

1. *Science and Humanism: Physics in our Time* (Canto Reprint: CUP, 1996) p. 117. On the finding of the sixth, or top, quark, see T. M. Liss and P. L. Lipton, *Scientific American* (September 1997) 36–41.

2. D/K B116 – Fragment B 116 in the standard edition of the original texts by H. Diels and W. Kranz, *Die Fragmente der Vorsokratiker*, 6th edn (Berlin, 1952), which including testimonia and spuria runs to over a hundred pages (hereafter D/K). The Stobaeus *Anthology* fragments are numbered B169–297; the less authoritative 'Democrates' collection B35–115. The most complete edition is S. Luria, *Democritea* (Leningrad, 1970), but this is not widely accessible. A small selection of original texts (unfortunately omitting some of Democritus' important ethical fragments), with introduction and commentary, may be found in M. R. Wright *The Presocratics* (Bristol: Bristol Classical Press, 1985).

    My English translations of fragments are contained in and cited from:

B   J. Barnes, *Early Greek Philosophy* (Harmondsworth: Penguin, 1987) [cited by page number]

C/M   P. Curd and R. D. McKirahan Jr, *A Presocratics Reader: Selected Fragments and Testimonia* (Indianapolis/ Cambridge: Hackett, 1995)

G/W   M. Gagarin and P. Woodruff, *Early Greek Political Thought from Homer to the Sophists* (Cambridge: CUP, 1995)

K/R/S G. S. Kirk, J. E. Raven and M. Schofield, *The Presocratic Philosophers*, 2nd edn (Cambridge: CUP, 1983) [also gives the original Greek]

P. F. Procopé, 'Democritus on Politics and the Care of the Soul: Appendix', *Classical Quarterly* 40 (1990) 21–45 [also gives the original Greek]

I have occasionally changed quoted passages, where the translation seemed to me unsatisfactory. Even more occasionally, I have provided my own.

3. Diogenes Laertius' *Lives of the Ancient Philosophers* (Democritus' brief life is at 9.34–49) is translated in the Loeb Classical Library (Harvard UP); cf. M. Gigante, 'Biografia e dossografia in Diogene Laerzio', *Elenchos* 7 (1986) 7–102 (on Democritus at p. 16). R. Ferwerda, 'Democritus and Plato', *Mnemosyne* 25 (1972) 337–78 reviews the ancient and modern literature bearing on the vexed question of the relationship of Plato's to Democritus' thought and so provides a useful overview in short compass of Democritus' multifarious *oeuvre*. An engagingly written recent monograph with comprehensive scope is J. Salem, *Démocrite. Grains de poussière dans un rayon de soleil* (Paris: Vrin, 1996). Other modern, general studies of Democritus that I have consulted include:

C. Bailey, *The Greek Atomists and Epicurus* (Oxford: OUP, 1928, repr. 1964) esp. 64–214

J. Barnes, *The Presocratic Philosophers* (London and New York: Routledge, 1982) esp. ch. 12 (342–77)

W. K. C. Guthrie, *A History of Greek Philosophy* II (Cambridge: CUP, 1965) ch. 8 'The Atomists of the Fifth Century' (382–507)

J. – P.Morel, *Démocrite et la recherche des causes* (Paris: Klincksieck, 1996)

H. Steckel, 'Demokritos', in *Pauly-Wissowas Real-*

Enzyklopaedie des classischen Altetums Supp. XII (1970) 191–223

Further specialist studies are cited under the appropriate sections below.

4. Gore Vidal, *Creation* (1981).

5. G. E. R. Lloyd, *Early Greek Science: Thales to Aristotle* (London: Chatto & Windus, 1970); id., 'The Social Background of Early Greek Philosophy and Science' (1972), repr. with new intro. in *Methods and Problems in Greek Science* (Cambridge: CUP, 1991) 121–40; id., 'Democracy, Philosophy, and Science in Ancient Greece', in J. Dunn (ed.), *Democracy: The Unfinished Journey 500 BC to AD 1993* (Oxford: OUP, 1992) 41–56; C. H. Kahn, 'Some Remarks on the Origins of Greek Science and Philosophy', in A. C. Bowen (ed.), *Science and Philosophy in Classical Greece* (New York: Garland, 1991) 1–10.

Physics and Epistemology

6. Besides the general works cited in note 3 see also D. J. Furley, *The Greek Cosmologists* 1 (Cambridge: CUP, 1987); id., 'Democritus', *Oxford Classical Dictionary*, 3rd edn (Oxford: OUP, 1996); id., 'Démocrite', in J. Brunschwig and G. Lloyd (eds), *Le Savoir grec* (Paris: Flammarion, 1996; Eng. trans. forthcoming, Harvard UP); P.-M. Morel, *Démocrite et la recherche des causes* (Paris: Klincksieck, 1996); D. O'Brien, *Theories of Weight in the Ancient World*, I: *Democritus: Weight and Size* (Leiden: Brill, 1981); C. C. W. Taylor, 'Pleasure, Knowledge and Sensation in Democritus', *Phronesis* 12 (1967) 6–27.

7. J. de Romilly, *The Great Sophists in Periclean Athens* (Oxford: OUP, 1992); cf. E. L. Hussey, *The Presocratic Philosophers* (London: Duckworth, 1972, repr. 1996).

Cosmology and Cosmography

8. Besides the general works cited in note 3 see also G. Vlastos, 'Equality and Justice in Early Greek Cosmologies' (1947), repr. in Vlastos, *Studies in Greek Philosophy* 1 (Princeton: Princeton UP, 1995), 57–88; D. J. Furley, *The Greek Cosmologists* 1 (Cambridge: CUP, 1987).

Anthropology and Sociology

9. Besides the general works cited in note 3 see also A. T. Cole, *Democritus and the Sources of Greek Anthropology* (Cleveland, OH: Western Reserve UP, 1967).

10. P. Cartledge, *The Greeks: A Portrait of Self and Others* (Oxford: OUP, rev. edn 1997).

Psychology and Medicine

11. Besides the general works cited in note 3 see also J. Gosling and C. Taylor, *The Greeks on Pleasure* (Oxford: OUP, 1982); C. H. Kahn, 'Democritus and the Origins of Moral Psychology', *American Journal of Philology* 106 (1985) 1–31; G. Lloyd, *The Revolutions of Wisdom: Studies in the Claims and Practice of Ancient Greek Science* (Berkeley: University of California Press, 1987).

Ethics and Politics

12. Besides the general works cited in note 3 and the article of Kahn (note 11) see also G. J. D. Aalders, 'The Political Faith of Democritus', *Mnemosyne* 1950: 302–13; C. Farrar, *The Origins of Democratic Thinking: The Invention of Politics in Classical Athens* (Cambridge: CUP, 1988); E. A. Havelock, *The Liberal Temper in Greek Politics* (New Haven: Yale UP,

1957) ch. 6, with the critique of P. A. Brunt reprinted in his *Studies in Greek History and Thought* (Oxford: OUP, 1993) 391–3; M. J. Nill, *Morality and Self-interest in Protagoras, Antiphon, and Democritus* (Leiden: Brill, 1985); J. Procopé, 'Democritus on Politics and the Care of the Soul', *Classical Quarterly* 39 (1989) 307–31; 40 (1990) 21–45; G. Vlastos, 'Ethics and Physics in Democritus' (1945–6), repr. in Vlastos, *Studies in Greek Philosophy* I (Princeton: Princeton UP, 1995) 328–50.

13. E. L. Hussey, 'Thucydidean History and Democritean Theory', in P. Cartledge and D. Harvey (eds), *CRUX: Essays in Greek History Presented to G. E. M. de Ste. Croix* (London: Duckworth, 1985) 118–38.

Reception: Democritus' Last Laugh

14. In M. A. Screech's translation and edition of Michel de Montaigne, *The Complete Essays* (London: Allen Lane, 1991) p. 339. According to one ancient doxographer, however, what Democritus laughed at was the folly of mankind in not realizing that in the cosmos all but atoms and the void were mere figments of convention.

15. Reproduced in e.g. (Sister) Wendy Beckett's *Odyssey* (London: BBC Books, 1993) 60–1.

16. L. G. Benakis (ed.), *Proceedings of the First International Congress on Demokritos* (Xanthi, 1984). See also notes 3 and 6.